Sense of Life

Pranav Gopalkrishna

Presentation by *BookLeaf Publishing*

Web: www.bookleafpub.com

E-mail: info@bookleafpub.com

ISBN: 9789357741811

First edition 2023

The Pale Grey Sky

(4 beats per line)

Look
Up and see the pale sky, and the
Merging damp clouds, with
Birds soaring so high,
Yet below the sombre shrouds. The

Day was full of brewing promise
Though a bit drab and cold. If
Grey turned blue, all would miss the
Rain the clouds foretold.

Wind

(2 beats per line)

In
Trillions particles stream, for
Aeons they've been flowing, slowing
Opposition even in a dream, like a
Superstition that's been growing. They col-

-lide against my skin, and pro-
-vide the feel of wind, and
Heal the sore mind within,
That was in a bore, pickled and tinned. They

Wash over like water, and
Gosh! It feels much sweeter. These
Breaths of the Sun's loveliest daughter make me
Slightly reel and teeter.

Flowers

(4 beats per line)

Tethered like a feather whether the weather is
fair or foul
Soon withering like a slithering snake pinned by
an owl.
Yet a whittling heart, brittle and dark, became a
lark, that
Soared, as it pored over the little bloom's
prettiness. Its

Delicate petals glow bright and strong in the
light,
Dainty and soft, held aloft, wavering but tight,
Around a round centre for which many critters
enter, bru-
-shing against the pollen, rushing to suckle the
nectar.

It's
Hapless, but my happiness comes not from its
weakness, but its
Prettiness, which is by no means a pettiness.
Aeons of evolution have found daintiness a
solution, and this
Sweetly captures the rapture of life's persistence,
per-

-sistence which I struggled to muster in a cluster
of dark clouds, which
Flocked my mind and rocked my peace with
stark doubts.
As I was wrestling with despair nestling, these e-
-phemeral treasures brought me a rare smile.

Rainfall

(4 beats per line)

Sprinkles from the heaven be-
-come torrents that leaven the weary
Soil, turning mud into mush, as
Countless droplets thud in a gush.
Sound of the touch of heaven's tears
That splinter like delicate glass, that
Fairies dropped while saying, "Cheers,"
Crying in regret, "Alas!"
But the occasion isn't of sorrow
Nor of angelic clumsiness. Nou-
-rishment like breadcrumbs in nests perme-
-ates the earth for days after tomorrow,
As all life consumes it, as
Little birds would the crumbs, each
Organism becomes invigo-
-rated as it subsumes it.

It
All began with a pale sky
Born of merging damp clouds, with
Birds soaring so high
Yet below these sombre shrouds. The
Day was full of brewing promise

Though a bit drab and cold, and if
Grey turned blue, all would miss the
Rain the clouds foretold. The day grew
Old, the blanket darkened.
Filled with icy drops, it wasn't warm.
Till then I'd see flocks of clouds swarm, and
Watch as I harkened for the
Faintest hint of thunder, as merging
Clouds coalesced as one. Soon enou-
-gh I started to wonder, "Why hasn't
It already begun?" Lo! A
Spark. Hark! A rumble. Oh, now
It's all going to tumble. The heavens will
Break, they can no more contain the
Bounty the sun had brought to them...

Pattering lightly, spreading with quick
Kisses onto every surface.
Battering slightly, threading with slick
Trickles these surfaces, in surpluses.
The purpose is to soak the dusty earth,
Bring out, polish, and renew its rusty worth
Expelling dearth and quelling thirst, as
Bazillion drops burst onto all of us head first,
then
All the fuss gets worse with a million things
drenched.
Smattering patter turns to roaring pour, the dirt
entrenched with

Shallow furrows taking raining cats and dogs
around rejoicing
Frogs, draining along the path, into slivers of
rivu-
-lets, the earth's own pretty, not-so-ostentatious
amu-
-lets, as the gracious sky showers the precious
beads for her to
String, which she does through many
mini-tributa-
-ries, as trees swish, leaves fluttering to
Ring, dripping wet, dropping dead leaves with
no obitua-
-ries, dropping twigs, flowers, and wild
Fruits, onto a tender mass of grass around my
Boots, onto buckling saplings and grappling
Roots, onto puddles and muddled soil, onto
Stone steps and the paved path, as the
Onslaught ceases as clouds uncoil, having
Given the earth a thorough bath. Flat
Dirt's impacted with the wet turmoil, with
Numerous tiny craters in the aftermath, re-
-sembling water in a simmering boil, but
Cool, its freshness emanating to the air. The
Earth quenched, packed ground unclenched, the
Sky's leaked dry, not a drop to spare.

Divided Attention

(2 beats per line)

"Hurray," cry my senses, at the
Touch of open air, as
Fresh as a flower's flair. But

As I walk along, the
World passes by me, as I sink
Into a reverie. My

Senses are divided, between
Skies, roads, and trees and my im-
-mersive fantasies.

Tree

(4 beats per line)

A
Bolt of lightning, rising from the
Earth, striking at every which way in a
Spurt, then freezing stiff and brown, giving
Birth to hanging drops of green.

Its splayed arms are uplifted to the
Sky, the firm lines never shifted, never
Will, unless abruptly rifted, till then they stay
Lifted to any light gifted. Dead matter's

Drifted away and around, lying un-
-sifted with green and yellow and mellow half
Brown, a carpet to the ground, in misshapen
Puddles with every drop apart. They

Dropped apart from the arms overhead.
There is no art to the manner they spread.
But the lines spread overhead follow a
Logic that guides every jagged stroke.

One, then few, then few more from each, ele-
-vating, widening out to reach the
Sky, grasping out to each
Ray of sunshine it can reach. The

Power gets captured in green, sending
Life coursing through the lightning bolts, no
Jolts come any more from their ends,
But the lightning is frozen no more. No

More is it a lightning, though,
Brightening nothing but the spirit.
Hear it rustle in the hustling breeze as it
Grows like lightening endlessly dulled and

Slowed, charged with freshness that had
Flowed, from when the rays first
Showed onto the emerging sprouts that
Sprang from energising dirt.

Snowy Mountains at Dusk

(2 beats per line)

Jagged edges and lofty ledges,
Ragged slopes for rugged sledges
Craggy tops and pointy maxima,
Shaggy woods framing the panorama,
Watching down with a hand on the rough bark,
there's a
Botchy town and a land in the growing dark.
The
Sun's still shining clear orange, and the
Light's outlining every fringe in a
Really bright tinge, like a slight singe a-
-long the snowy rocky sides only good for
knocky rides
Crocky slides are showing now as moonlight's
glowing about,
Cracked, snagged, here and there, with
Winding paths everywhere.
They're not really ominous, though looming and
enormous,
Silhouetted guardians, whose corners are all
hardy ends.
Absolutely unperturbed, they attend to none,
Each an ancient phenomenon,

Heaved up from the very earth,
By the Earth, no pain no mirth, as
Nature's workings are indifferent, can
Be indifferently magnificent, as
Magnificently they form the world, from the
The starry sky to slender vines that are twirled a-
-round the trees in this chilly wood, at the
Mountain's foot, from where I could
See the frosty peak pierce the sky,
Among twinkling stars fierce and high.

My Piece of the Sky

(2 beats per line)

A
Piece of the sky has
Fallen onto the sheet, has
Seeped and spread, in and throughout,
Clear and complete. I

Gaze into its hue, as I
Carefully hold it still.
Nature paints the sky, but this
Piece is mine to fill. I

Could just imitate, and
Speckle the blue with white,
Dab it with some grey, or
Brush it pale and light. I

Could let loose some birds, reaching the
Clouds or heading away. I could
Bring an airplane to life, dashing a-
-cross in a straight ray. Or

I could split my thoughts asunder,
Into bits and elements, cre-
-ate something anew, through
Fresh rearrangements. I'll

Let my fancy play, and give
Way to thoughts absurd. Maybe
One would gain wings enough to
Take off like a bird. It's

Just a little piece of blue, but a
Doorway need not be so grand. Its
Possibilities, vast as the sky, yet
Within the reach of my drawing hand.

Melody

(6 beats per line)

Weaving from one plane to a-
-nother, in one whole chain,
One sole train unravelling
On, travelling past, not too

Fast… on and a-
-way… into new
Paths… maybe few
Hearts… as the

Rails keep shivering, its
Trails still quivering, as the
Patterns arise and transform, as the
Train goes on, weaving its way into
Something more beautiful, hued with full
melodies
Coming together as one… As

New threads are spun, awesome as
Saturn's rings, but patterns swing
Not just around, as sounds take the
Bounds of motion on ahead, as
Notes tread in a train, un-
-folding creation until the very
End.

Practice and Performance

(2 beats per line)

Sounds emerge from behind the board, whose
Keys I manipulate gloriously, mere
Sounds intertwine harmoniously, and
Follow in a structure melodiously. I had

Struggled to to bring the music out, as a
Painter does to get his strokes right,
Concentrating with all my might, to
Make the score sing through the night. At

Times my fingers fail me,
Slipping a key or missing a note
Dismally as a lopsided boat,
Sounding worse than a goat with a sore throat.
Per-

-fection stained is perfection lost,
Be the stain however little.
Even grandness could be belittled, and
Presentation's flair would whittle away, brittle.

Once it is laid out, though,
Wordless songs flow into the ears,
Every phrase longs to express, as it nears
Beauty, in the many forms it appears.

Motorised Locomotion

(4 beats per line)

The
Forces of nature harnessed and controlled, the
Fiery potential of ancient fuels rea-
-lised and released into closed chambers, cre-
-ating bursts of motion woven
Into a circle, whose movement unfolds
Onto the path, taking me on and a-
-way in an unswerving ray,
Heavy as a boulder yet fast as the wind.

Through
Forces of nature harnessed and controlled, the
Cold, dead matter is given life,
Given a form exuding purpose,
Glorious purpose to move, to hold and pro-
-pel itself with power and poise, to
Carry with it its precious load, to
Carry living minds and their wealth,
Dangerously fast, yet safe in its grasp.

Creation

(4 beats per line)

A
Tangle of mass lies before me to
Show me what is possible. I
Bring my hands, apply my mind to sup-
-ply what I find to the crucible.

It's like pulling from the tangle a thread to
Weave order from chaos,
Using muscles and a thinking head to
Bear the effort for the payoffs. To ma-

-terialise my work, never do I
Shirk from this exertion, to
Mould and batter this matter, bind and
Align it into an assertion against dis-

-order, asserting through its form,
"Here I stand till I break apart.
Entropy may be the norm,
Yet I'll stay as a work of art." My

Mental heat shapes a spirit that es-
-capes through the structure, not like
Blood through a rupture, but like
Beauty through a sculpture. The

Force of purpose was the
Source of this heat. The
Course of my action sprang from
This, as a stream from a spring, a

Spring that rose from within, from
Want and desire. Cre-
-ation only did begin when I
Channelled this fluid fire,

Feeding it to my crucible for
Forcible heat to spring,
To melt down the fodder to re-
-order it into a thing, an

Object of beauty and use, the
Fruits of my labour. The
Roots of man's progress are the
Shoots of the seeds of his thought.

Look at the rising skyline
Shine under the blazing sun,
Look at the wheels over roads, under
Loads too massive for anyone.

Watch those ships brave the vast oceans, and
That one swimming through the clouds, see the
Words encoding emotions from a
Time covered in shrouds.

All this forged in the heat of the
Seat of the mind, like
These words you're hearing now,
Searing with every rhyme.

Integration

(2 beats per line)

A
Force at the core, that's a
Door to the course of a
Realisation of
Effort and being. A
Thread going around but bou-
-nd by a fountainhead, the
Kind that brings melodies
Into harmony. Though the
Voices are many, they form
One symphony, whole
As an epiphany, ever
True to the theme. The
Source and intent are a guiding
Force that is bent toward a
True purpose, be it to
Live or sew a seam. A

Dysfunctional body is a
Shoddy formation.
So would things be rendered, if
Order were surrendered to
Chaos, where the way's lost, for

Lack of rhyme and reason, a trea-
-son to any purpose, as the
Conception is purged.
Elements not needed are an
Irrational splurge. What
Needs to be heeded is the
Rational urge toward a
Structure that shapes a
Spirit that escapes by
Being given a form, like
Beauty through a sculpture.

Pieces of knowledge
All edge toward a
Girder, fleshed out of
Steel and concrete,
Integration of the
Abstract and concrete,
That a mind would bind
Into understan-
-ding right and firm, again-
-st hurdles and squirms, the ter-
-ms stating my views need to
Be held by understan-
-ding of what, how, and why,
No sly evasions;
Want your mind cracking at the
Slightest abrasions?

The Greatest Gift

(8 beats per line)

Lo and behold! Here's the world before you. It
e-
-xisted before, and will persist beyond you. No-
-thing's apart from it; even you're a part of it,
even
If you feel, perhaps, that you're the start of it.
You

See all around you that things are what they are,
Everything that is, from the rock to the star.
All things abound, there is much that surrounds,
but
You can grasp that which leads to thoughts
profound, the

Essence, the abstraction, the algebra of
knowledge, the
Means whereby you'd more than just perceive
and allege, the
Means whereby you'd know the many from the
one, grasp
The plurality of all things under the sun,

Bring the infinite into the range of perception,
In a single word hold an immense conception.
This is the one great gift of humanity,
Learn so you may flourish, not fall into insanity.

Bad Premises

(2 beats per line)

When I was younger, my i-
-magination ran wilder, but
It fed a hunger for
Making reality milder.
Rocks were scarcely hewn and
Shaped with wise effort,
Sweat was rarely strewn, as I tried
To dream away any hurt. The

Premise was simple, "i-
-magine, thus be." Seems
Cute as a dimple, but is a
Catastrophe. See, in
Daydreams I'm a god, but re-
-ality has its absolutes, and
There is no reward for
Leaving the mind destitute, for-
-saking rationality for the
Sake of avoiding the strain of con-
-fusion in reality, which was
Driving me insane. What

Really matters in life? What to
Do in my strife? How to
Cope with these emotions engul-
-fing me like an ocean?

Worst of all, my premise was bad,
First of all, it wasn't fit to use.
But… it was all I had
With… wisdom scarce and loose.
This… is what I mean, when
I say I was messed up,
Addled before I was a teen, by a
Premise that stank yet dressed up. The

Premise reeked of a lot else, like
Those decrepit hotels.
It was a veritable monster, co-
-nstantly upholstered, with
This fancy stuff, and that lacy bluff,
While the structure was rotten, crumbling.
Finally it fell, and that hurt, but
I was freed from the shit and dirt. My
Notions of truth were sabotaged, it's my
Mind that was barraged, by i-
-deas of perfection that make no sense, but they
Were an abasement of truth, beware hence.

Deepest Value

(4 beats per line)

What's good, and what's evil? The line's not
Sharp as a needle, so we will set a
Standard that is true, head to the
Deepest value, as the
Scientist reached the atom, so much of the
World he could now fathom! So
Come with what you know, let's go to the
Core from where all values flow. Oh

Man, you know, what can be but my life, which
I'd hold dear, in joy or strife. I'd
Fight every knife that threatens to blight it, Ig-
-nite all things that lessen and slight it, be-
-cause throughout my life I exist.
One couldn't be more of a realist. If
Ever to me it doesn't matter, it's
Then that my will shall shatter. So

What's good and evil, can you say? The
Line seems blurred, but there is a way. Set a
Standard, not stolen nor crafted, but true. May
Life be the standard, the deepest value.

Freedom

(4 beats per line)

She
Stands, not weak nor withered, from the a-
-byss of despair she's delivered. A
Storm rages outside, yet in her
Eyes is something fiercer, de-
-fiance in her being, as if no
Pain should dare to pierce her. Her

Withheld expression couldn't
Hold back her radiance, wouldn't
Hold back the joy, the furious
Joy coursing through her veins, her
Posture, still and steady, as if to
Keep her hold on the reins.

All my pity's vaporised;
Such a being deserves none. No
Feeling so pathetic for a
Living drop of the sun! Her
Grey tunic is but a wisp of a
Cloud coming undone. "I'm

Free," she says quietly, but I
Can't imagine otherwise, as if
This were an axiom that from her
Being one would surmise. Is
This the blooming of volition that in
Myself I could realise?

Joy of Achievement

(2 beats per line)

The
Man climbed the mountain, re-
-joiced in the fruits of his deeds. The
Strengthening exertion, the beauty around him -
These were his only heartfelt needs.

Joy sprang in a fountain, almost
Burst to make him bleed. Its pul-
-sation began to pound him, from
Pain and despair he was freed.

Such joy I would count in my
Reasons to proceed with my
Efforts, such that crowned him king of the
Peak, adorned with a sweat bead.